# Six Sigma Healthcare

By Ade Asefeso MCIPS MBA

Second Edition

ISBN-13: 978-1499389555
ISBN-10: 1499389558

Publisher: AA Global Sourcing Ltd
Website: http://www.aaglobalsourcing.com

# Table of Contents

# Disclaimer

This publication is designed to provide competent and reliable information regarding the subject matter covered. However, it is sold with the understanding that the author and publisher are not engaged in rendering professional advice. The authors and publishers specifically disclaim any liability that is incurred from the use or application of contents of this book.

If you purchased this book without a cover you should be aware that this book may have been stolen property and reported as "unsold and destroyed" to the publisher. In this case neither the author nor the publisher has received any payment for this "stripped book."

# Dedication

This book is dedicated to the hundreds of thousands of incredible souls in the world who have weathered through the up and down of recent recession.

To my family and friends who seems to have been sent here to teach me something about who I am supposed to be. They have nurtured me, challenged me, and even opposed me.... But at every juncture has taught me!

This book is dedicated to my lovely boys, Thomas, Michael and Karl. Teaching them to manage their finance will give them the lives they deserve. They have taught me more about life, presence, and energy management than anything I have done in my life.

# Chapter 1: Introduction

Concerns about the quality of healthcare in the United States have recently emerged from many different quarters. A presidential commission concluded that quality problems often cause impaired health. United Kingdom's Government also concluded that "serious and widespread quality problems exist throughout the National Health Service (NHS)".

Healthcare quality is a prominent and recurring topic in the nationwide debates in both the UK and US about the perceived adverse effects of managed care.

In this book, we will explores critical underlying causes of quality problems, discusses some of the most salient obstacles to improvement, and suggests the components of an effective strategy to increase the pace and scope of quality improvement in the delivery system.

The Institute of Medicine's definition of quality has proved of enduring usefulness. "Quality is the extent to which health services for individuals and populations increase the likelihood of desired health outcomes and are consistent with current professional knowledge" (Institute of Medicine 1990). Many reliable and valid measures of quality have been developed, building on this definition. In general, valid quality measures assess either processes (diagnostic or therapeutic interventions) or outcomes (health states that people experience). Process

7

measures are valid quality measures when their relation to important health outcomes has been proved. The frequency with which heart attack survivors receive beta blockers is a valid quality measure because these medications improve survival in this clinical situation.

For a health outcome to be a valid quality measure, it must be related conclusively to a process or group of processes that can be modified to improve the outcome. Thus, the number of babies born with HIV infection is a valid measure of quality of care because treatment in the prepartum period with zidovudine has been proved to reduce the transmission of infection from mother to infant. Cardiogenic shock, on the other hand, has not been proved to respond to specific treatment regimens; therefore, deaths from that cause are not valid measures of healthcare quality.

## The Six Sigma Challenge

Many careful research studies have used valid measures of quality to investigate the nature and magnitude of specific quality problems. Quality problems may be classified into three categories; overuse, underuse, and misuse. As the research literature makes clear, quality problems of all three varieties abound in American medicine. The majority of these problems are not rare, unpredictable, or inevitable concomitants of the delivery of complex, modern healthcare. Rather, they are frighteningly common, often predictable, and frequently preventable. Viewed by those companies that have committed themselves to the most advanced

8

applications of industrial quality management, the magnitude of the failures or quality defects in the provision of healthcare must seem stupefying. A few examples will highlight this contrast.

Motorola and General Electric, among others, have set reliability goals for the manufacture of their products and services that they describe as the quest for Six Sigma Quality. Motorola invented this strategy, which is named for a statistical measure of variation (the standard deviation of a normal distribution). Simply put, adopting the goal of Six Sigma quality means setting tolerance limits for defective products at such high levels that fewer than 3.4 defects occur per million units (or opportunities). These limits are set to include all observations within 6 standard deviations of the mean. Setting tolerance limits at lower levels of sigma results in higher rates of defects. Advocates of this approach to quality claim that it works just as well in service industries as in manufacturing

A defect rate may be defined in whatever terms are sensible for the process that is being improved. It may refer to the number of parts (per million produced) for an aircraft engine that fail to meet all the mechanical specifications for inclusion in the finished product. A defect may also be defined as the number of telephone calls from customers that go unanswered after three (or four or five) rings (per million calls).

In healthcare, defects might be defined as the number of two-year-olds who are not completely immunized (per million two-year-olds in the population). Another might be the number of pregnant women failing to receive prenatal care in the first trimester (per million pregnancies). A third might be the number of patients with clinical depression who are not diagnosed or well treated (per million patients with depression).

Simply setting the goal of reducing defects to 3.4 per million (or fewer) does not guarantee that it will be achieved. Allied-Signal, which began its Six Sigma program in 1994, claims that most of its manufacturing plants operate in the range of 3.5 to 4 sigma and that three model factories have already achieved 6 sigma levels of quality. General Electric improved from 3 to 3.5 sigma in the first 22 months of its program, reducing the average frequency of defects from 67,000 to 23,000 per million. Although this strategy was first applied to manufacturing processes, Motorola, General Electric, and others have extended its applications to aspects of their businesses that involve direct customer services.

## Underlying Causes of Quality Problems

Why do we have such serious quality problems in healthcare? Some have suggested lack of information as the main reason. If only physicians knew the latest scientific evidence concerning the effectiveness or ineffectiveness of specific interventions (and if only there was more of it), the right things would get done more often (and the wrong things would be more often avoided). I believe that the underlying forces at work are far more complex and much more difficult to remediate. In addition, the fundamental causes

10

differ, depending on which class of quality problem one considers.

# Chapter 2: The History of Six Sigma

Six Sigma as a powerful business strategy has been around for over twenty years and has grown exponentially in healthcare industry during the past years. As a process performance improvement methodology, Six Sigma is viewed today as a disciplined, systematic, measurement-based and data-driven approach to reduce process variation. This powerful management strategy combines improved metrics and cook-book methodology to reduce defects or mistakes or errors in processes and thereby strengthening a company's market position and enhancing the financial impact to the bottom-line.

In manufacturing, it is quite possible to reduce or even eliminate (in some cases) most of human variability through automation. In healthcare industry, the delivery of patient care is largely a human process, and hence the causes of variability are often difficult to identify and quantify.

Six Sigma was first developed by Motorola in the late 1980s. It has been extensively used within companies such as General Electric (GE), Allied Signal (former Honeywell), ABB, Texas Instruments, Caterpillar, Sony, Toshiba, City Bank, Bank of America, JP Morgan Chase to name a few here. Sigma is a Greek letter used to describe process variability or in mathematical terms, standard deviation of a random variable. A number of times Sigma indicates the amount of defects that are likely to occur in a given process (manufacturing, service or transactional). For example, a 3 sigma process has a defect rate of 6.7% whereas a Six Sigma process has less than 4 defects per million opportunities. Defects in processes cause increase in costs due to scrap, rework, repair, re-test and so on. The following are some of the typical characteristics of Six Sigma.

- Emphasises a data-driven methodology.
- Places a strong emphasis on customer needs and expectations (in Six sigma context these are called Critical-to-Quality characteristics (CTQs).
- Focuses on elimination of defects or errors in processes due to unacceptable process variation.
- Offers a structured approach to get into the root causes of problems using the DMAIC (Define-Measure-Analyse-Improve-Control) methodology.
- Integration of powerful statistical and non-statistical tools in a sequential manner within the DMAIC methodology.
- Places a greater emphasis on hard-dollar savings from projects which are aligned with strategic objectives of organisation's business.

## Six Sigma versus Total Quality Management (TQM)

Six Sigma is often criticised as "an old wine in a new bottle".

There are five aspects of the Six Sigma business improvement strategy that are not emphasised in Total Quality Management (TQM) and possibly many other quality improvement initiatives of the past.

Six Sigma places a very clear focus on the bottom-line impact in financial or monetary terms. A Six Sigma project will not be approved by the Project Champion (who is responsible for assigning projects) unless the bottom-line impact has been identified.

As Six Sigma is a data-driven methodology to problem solving, a Six Sigma team uses measurements to analyse problems and thereby improve the patient care process. This measurement is the sigma quality level with which the core healthcare processes are currently operating.

This sigma quality level of a process provides a baseline performance for process improvement activities.

Six Sigma has been very successful in integrating both the human and process aspects of improvement. Here the process aspects include process stability, process capability, etc. whereas the human aspects include teamwork, customer focus, cultural change, leadership etc.

The Six Sigma methodology (DMAIC) creates a sense of urgency by emphasising rapid completion of projects in a very stringent time framework of between 4 and 6 months. No improvement process uses DMAIC as effectively as Six Sigma does.

Six Sigma utilises a very healthy infrastructure of champions, Master Black belts, Black belts, Green belts and Yellow belts that lead, deploy and implement the methodology. The champions provide resources and keep the project focused on the business need; remove barriers or obstacles (if any) encountered by the Black belts during the project execution and get involved in the selection of Black belts for project execution.

The Master Black belts is the technical expert providing training, coaching and counselling for the Black belts and Green belts. The Black belts work full time on projects which on average should bring at least $175,000 to the bottom-line of the organisation. The Green belts carry out small projects in their own work place and generally work part time on projects. The Yellow belts in many cases are process owners and assist Black belts and Green belts in data gathering and collection methods.

# Chapter 3: Six Sigma Methodology in Healthcare

For decades the U.S. healthcare industry has been operating on its own way ignoring emerging factors such as competition, patient safety, skyrocketing healthcare cost, liability, malpractice insurance cost and use of (Diagnosis-related group) DRG for Medicare and insurance payment. However, as these factors became more prevalent and competition within the industry intensified, many U.S. hospitals have been becoming increasingly aware of the critical needs of controlling the operating costs and meet and even exceeds the expectations of patient care quality.

In current competitive environment, many healthcare organizations are taking steps to ensure that they are providing the "absolute best care at the lowest possible costs". However, many hospital administrators still have to learn how to lower operating costs without compromising on providing consistent good quality patient care.

In 1993, 44% of 1,083 hospitals surveyed in the U.S. were embracing some kind of quality management approach such as CQI (Continuous quality improvement), Kaizen, and TQM (Total Quality Management) to improve healthcare quality.

## Six Sigma DMAIC Quality Improvement Model

The Six Sigma quality improvement model as applied at Motorola, Inc refers to the five step process problem solving approach known as DMAIC (Define, Measure, Analyze, Improve and Control) as explained below.

**Define:** this step defines who the customers are, what the customers want, the process capabilities, and provides objectives for project-based improvement efforts.

**Measure:** this step measures the quality characteristics that reflects improvement in customer satisfaction and product performance and provides the metrics of data on which the improvement efforts will be based.

**Analyze:** in this step, data collected in previous steps are analyzed using analytical tools such as Pareto analysis, process flow diagram, fish-bone diagram, statistical process control charts, for identifying necessary design and process modifications for achieving customer satisfaction and performance objectives.

**Improve:** in this step resources are allocated so that design and process modifications needed for improvement can be implemented.

**Control:** in this step the process is monitored using quality management tools such as Pareto charts, and statistical process control charts to ensure that the performance improvements are maintained.

The Six Sigma process is highly measurement and data driven. Data has to be gathered to determine the baseline performance of a process in order to validate that an improvement has been made. Decisions are made on statistics and facts, rather than instinct or past history. Six Sigma projects can be lead by Black Belts or Green Belts experts who are trained for quality problem solving. The Master Black Belt usually serves as advisors to the project leaders while local champions promote Six Sigma in their organizations. All of these roles require extensive training to become familiar with the tools of Six Sigma. Six Sigma projects that focus on improving/solving existing quality problems follow the process of DMAIC (Define, Measure, Analyze, Improve, and Control) as described above. While projects that involve developing a new product, process or procedure follow the DFSS (Design for Six Sigma) process that focus on meeting customer needs and expectation, on time and on budget.

## Six Sigma approach to healthcare industry

The challenge for healthcare industry to benefit from the use of Six Sigma is paramount. Patient care significantly involves human element as compared to machine elements, in which the variability is subtle and very difficult to quantify. Therefore, challenge in adopting Six Sigma approach to healthcare is to find a way to leverage the data from Six Sigma to drive human behaviour. Success will come only when the

Six Sigma technical strategy is combined with a cultural strategy for change acceleration and a sound operational mechanism.

There are usually four metrics (indicators) that can be used by singly or in combination to define level of performance of a healthcare organization. These metrics are service level, service cost, customer satisfaction, and clinical excellence. While these metrics are applicable in healthcare organizations, they are also very difficult to apply in a healthcare setting. Despite the challenges in using Six Sigma in the healthcare industry, many hospitals within the healthcare industry are beginning to use Six Sigma approach to improve patients' satisfaction.

The Six Sigma methodology works quite well in healthcare processes. Six Sigma projects in healthcare industry are focused on direct care delivery, administrative support and financial administration. Six Sigma projects can be executed in the following healthcare processes.

- Increasing capacity in X-ray room.
- Reducing turn-around time in preparing medical reports.
- Improving patient satisfaction at ER.
- Reducing bottle necks in emergency department.
- Reducing cycle time in various inpatient and outpatient diagnostic areas.
- Reducing the number of medical errors and hence enhancing patient safety.
- Increasing the accuracy of laboratory results.

- Increasing the accuracy of billing processes and thereby reducing the number of billing errors.
- Improving bed availability across various departments in hospitals.
- Reducing the number of post-operative wound infections and related wound problems.
- Increasing surgical capacity.
- Reducing length of stay in ER.
- Reducing inventory levels.
- Improving patient registration accuracy, and so on.

## Critical Success Factors (CSFs) of Six Sigma in Healthcare Industry

Like manufacturing processes, CSFs play a crucial role in the implementation of Six Sigma projects within the healthcare industry. The leaders of healthcare industry should consider the application of Six Sigma from the perspective of improving the quality and capability of current processes as well as the ability of processes to deliver patient care and safety. The following list of CSFs are absolutely imperative for the successful development and deployment of Six Sigma in a hospital environment.

1. Uncompromising Top Management Support and Commitment.

Applying Six Sigma in a healthcare sector is not easy, and if senior management team is not on board, it is almost certainly a formula for failure. The deployment of Six Sigma should begin with a two day broad overview of Six Sigma business strategy for the senior management team, ensuring buy-in and commitment for the implementation.

Six Sigma project champions responsible for identifying and overseeing projects must be carefully chosen before the training program. In order to buy-in senior management support and commitment, it is also essential to select projects which are tied to strategic business focus.

2. Formation of Six Sigma infrastructure and the appropriate Training

The selection of right people is crucial for the execution of Six Sigma projects. Once the Six Sigma infrastructure is defined with the help of a Six Sigma consultant with adequate experience from service industry, training may begin. The project champions should receive a good overview of Six Sigma fundamentals and the skills required for project selection, project prioritisation, and project scoping and project execution.

The Black belts must receive four weeks of intensive training, one week each month for four months. The focus of the training must be on the execution of Six Sigma projects and the required tools and techniques for problem solving.

The Black belts should work on two Six Sigma projects as part of their certification process. Each

Black belt is expected to spend at least 80% of their time on Six Sigma projects. The Green belts must receive two weeks of training. Green belts may work part-time and are expected to select a project from their own processes at the work place. They may also get involved with those projects which are executed by Black belts.

3. Project selection and the associated financial returns to the bottom-line

Potential Six Sigma projects within a healthcare setting may relate to operational processes such as billing, registration or work flow or they may involve clinical procedures such as medication administration. When identifying and prioritising projects in a healthcare industry, the first consideration should be the customer and knowing the Critical-to-Quality characteristics (CTQs) that drives the project. The customer in this context may be the patient, physician, nursing staff, department manager or other stakeholder, depending on the process being reviewed. The following tips may be useful while selecting potential Six Sigma projects in healthcare industry.

- Projects must be aligned with critical hospital issues, patient care issues and strategic objectives of the business.
- Projects must be feasible to execute from a resource and data standpoint.
- Project objectives must be clear to everyone involved in the project.
- Ensure that projects can be completed on time.

- Ensure that a tollgate review must be performed at every stage of the Six Sigma methodology.
- Select those projects which have the ability to show measurable improvements in quality, cost and timeliness parameters.

## Some Common Barriers and Challenges in the implementation of Six Sigma within Healthcare Industry

There are several barriers and challenges lurking below the surface for healthcare industry for consideration before the implementation and deployment of Six Sigma business strategy. The first and foremost challenge is the initial investment in Six Sigma Belt System training. The absence or difficulty to obtain the baseline data on process performance is another major challenge while applying Six Sigma in healthcare sector. There will be lots of data available in the healthcare sector, however, most of the time these data are not readily available for its analysis. For healthcare industry, it is often a struggle to identify processes which can be measured in terms of defects or errors per million opportunities. Another barrier to Six Sigma deployment in healthcare industry is the psychology of the workforce. Last but not the least, it is important to present recommendations using the business language rather than the statistical language.

Although Six Sigma has been used by world class companies for several years with immense success, its application in healthcare sector is still in its infancy.

Appropriately implemented, Six Sigma clearly produces benefits in terms of laboratory and medication error reduction, improved patient care, etc. Some of the early successful applications of Six Sigma in healthcare have resulted in a reduction of surgical inventory costs, reduction in length of stay at Emergency Room and an improvement in patient satisfaction. The success stories of Six Sigma are rapidly growing, all touting the impact of this powerful and rigorous methodology to problem solving.

We believe that Six Sigma as a business strategy allows healthcare sector to deliver a truly high class service to patients. Think of the true impact that Six Sigma could have if we focus on the core issues of healthcare and improving the quality of lives of patients. In our opinion, the application of Six Sigma in healthcare industry will continue to grow, especially in the UK and the US over the next five years or so. As with all improvement strategies all it takes is a couple of brave leaders willing to take the right course and confront resistance to core issues once and for all.

# Chapter 4: Guidelines for Six Sigma Healthcare Project Selection

Once a healthcare organization has decided that Six Sigma can be an effective approach to improving the many services it delivers, the question then becomes how does it know where to start implementing the methodology's statistical process tools.

Process issues or variability in healthcare may exist around a particular piece of technology, within a certain department or care area, along service lines such as cardiology, or even across the entire organization. Potential Six Sigma projects may relate to operational processes such as billing, registration or workflow, or they may involve clinical procedures such as medication administration or Intensive Care Unit protocols. But do all roads lead to success and can an organization travel them all simultaneously? While the organization undoubtedly has multiple priorities that must be weighed and kept in balance and many stakeholders to satisfy; there are some basic guidelines for Six Sigma project selection within a healthcare organization.

## First Consideration Should Be the 'Customer'

When reviewing and prioritizing the opportunities in an organization, the first consideration should be the "customer" and as we mentioned in the previous chapter knowing the CTQs (critical to quality elements) that will drive the project. The customer in a healthcare project may be the patient, physician, nursing staff, administration, department manager or other stakeholder, depending on the process being reviewed.

It is also important to understand the complexity of the problem to be addressed and how many variables must be dealt with. If the problem is fairly complex with a number of measurable response variables, it may be a viable candidate for Six Sigma. Not every issue rises to the level of Six Sigma rigor for a solution, however; there are change management tools such as change acceleration process (CAP) and Work-out that have been effectively applied in cases that simply need greater direction, facilitation and consensus building with the right people involved.

## Common Characteristics of Six Sigma Projects

While each healthcare organization has specific needs and issues to resolve, the most successful Six Sigma projects usually share common characteristics:

- Feasibility from a resource and data standpoint.
- Unambiguous parameters and clearly defined goals.
- Alignment with critical hospital issues and strategic initiatives.
- Provision of visible benefits for the customer.
- Inclusion of a Green Belt or Black Belt working within the project area.
- Ability to show measurable improvement.
- Linkage with other projects for a combined effect.

- Personal connection for the project leader.

The human side of performance improvement; especially in a service industry such as healthcare must not be overlooked. Since Six Sigma requires commitment and willingness to change, it is important that those who support or participate in the project recognize that a problem exists and that a solution must be found through objective methods.

**Some Additional Tips for Beginners**

For an organization or team undertaking its first wave of Six Sigma projects as part of a training or improvement initiative, there are a few additional tips to keep in mind:

- Make sure the problem is controllable and the solution is to your benefit.
- Keep it simple; save eliminating world hunger for your second project!
- Select an issue that will produce immediate and tangible benefits to the organization; early and visible wins provide momentum.
- Choose something with boundaries; both in time and effort.
- Try to select a project that has a comprehensive, rigorous data tracking system in place (usually financial or operational data).
- Choose something that is non-controversial and won't eliminate jobs.
- Choose something with an element of fun; it is a long road.

To help keep efforts focused in the right areas, it is also advisable to use some form of prioritization matrix. It is important to weight the key CTQs with well-defined operational definitions for scoring. The following matrix was developed to help one health system prioritize and select a project within cardiac services, by weighting factors such as the impact on clinical excellence, physician satisfaction and financial impact.

At one hospital in Canada, the QFD (quality function deployment) tool was used to gain consensus on the best area to focus on for Six Sigma improvement in the emergency room (ER). As indicated in patient satisfaction scores, they had opportunities in every part of the ER. The goal was to determine the project that would produce the greatest impact.

In this instance, the hospital team prioritized the CTQs; (critical to quality) gathered from interviews, survey data and then determined the strength of the relationship in addressing the CTQs by ranking again to the focus areas. In this hospital, Six Sigma Master Black Belts found the relationship matrix tool to be useful for examining key criteria Sources for Six Sigma Project Ideas:

- Quality function deployment.
- Customer dashboards.
- Surveys and scorecards.
- Day of surgery add-on rates.
- Active beta themes.
- Other projects available for leverage.
- Brainstorming.

- Analysis of critical processes.
- Discussions with customer.
- Financial analysis.
- Internal problems.
- Linkage to strategic priorities.
- Ability to complete the project within 6 to 9 months (or tighter timeframe, depending on situation).
- Potential financial benefit.
- Ease of data availability.
- Not already being worked on.
- Impact is quantifiable.
- Passionate sponsor.
- Needs analysis in some depth.
- No obvious solution.
- Translation or "spread" opportunities.
- Significant gap between current and desirable performance (including meeting regulatory specifications).
- Sense of urgency to address the problem.

"We worked with the key executives to give each factor a priority," The Master Black Belt Andy said, "usually a scale of 1-5 for each, and then rated a list of suggested project ideas against each of these (high/medium/low)... multiplying the two, adding it all up to give a relative score to each project idea. Then we did a 'gut check' once we rated them all to see which floated to the top. This approach helps to objectively steer the discussion and decisions."

Healthcare Organizations should take time at the beginning to make sure improvement projects are carefully selected and will drive direct, measurable benefits for the institution. While one can learn a great deal from other organizations, it is important to take one's own unique situation into consideration. For example, while a cycle time project related to CT (computerized tomography) scans may be perfect for one institution and deliver improved revenue and greater satisfaction, another may not have sufficient patient demand to warrant concentration in this area. Knowing what to look for and having a few tips and tools for finding the right answers can help to steer Six Sigma projects in the right direction.

# Chapter 5: Lean Six Sigma Signifies a Fundamental Break in Tradition

Lean Six Sigma signifies a fundamental break in tradition within Western management ideology. It also enables the healthcare industry several basic and standardized solutions for many of their organizational and procedural issues.

Traditionally, western ideology consisted of a few basic and simplified assumptions. First, the assumption was made that there needed to be a separation between thinking and doing in order to effectively and efficiently perform certain procedures. Defects were inevitable and almost impossible to avoid. Organizations need to be designed in a hierarchical manner with chains of commands and various other segments. Lastly, keeping inventory was necessary although time consuming but is important in buffering fluctuations in production and vital in producing products and services to the ever in-demand market.

Lean Six Sigma enables the healthcare industry several basic and standardized solutions for many of their organizational and procedural issues. For instance, it enhances visual management procedures and reduces the complexity and time of processes. This version of Six Sigma is highly implemented due to its strength in enabling persons to incorporate certain procedures with its main focus on the patient.

In 2003, this methodology was applied to the healthcare industry led and previously tested by the Standford Hospital and Clinics. It was also implemented in several Red Cross Hospitals. Some hospitals may have been currently using another type of quality assurance system and then implemented this process in its place. These hospitals recorded that before using Six Sigma, several operations that had been standardized by another quality assurance system lacked framework within the organization. In addition, general tracking, coordination, support and project management were not being focused on. Incidentally, project leaders recorded several problems which were later successfully solved by the program.

Six Sigma implementation is a quick process taking up at most two to three sessions widely spaced, frequent practical trials within the hospital settings and random exams. By using it, a great number of factors and issues were unearthed including inconsistencies in tracking temporary employees, managing operating theatre start times, and maintaining hospital equipment, machines, and similar devices just to name a few. These were just some issues of concern brought up. With the help of 6 Sigma they were able to find the root of each problem and present several methods of repairing them or implementing new procedures in order to quickly complete them. Lean Six Sigma can be used in various ways within the healthcare industry and has continued to enable healthcare professionals to offer sound and efficient care to the human populace.

# Chapter 6: National Health Service and Lean Six Sigma

The United Kingdom's National Health Service (NHS) is the largest healthcare system in the world. Its annual budget is for 2012/13 is around £108.9 billion and it employs more than 1.7m people. Of those, just under half are clinically qualified, including, 39,780 general practitioners (GPs), 370,327 nurses, 18,687 ambulance staff and 105,711 hospital and community health service (HCHS) medical and dental staff.

Only the Chinese People's Liberation Army, the Wal-Mart supermarket chain and the Indian Railways directly employ more people.

The NHS is in the middle of a programme of transformational change. The aim is to provide a health and healthcare service that meets the life-long needs of the citizens of United Kingdom. Ambitious goals have been set to reduce the burden of disease and improve outcomes of care to reduce hospital admissions by supporting people with long term conditions in managing their own care and by providing preventative, community-based services; to improve clinical quality and safety; to improve access to care, remove health inequalities and eliminate delays.

This mission requires multiple improvement strategies on multiple fronts. On one level, it requires nothing less than fundamental redesign of the healthcare system. At another level, it needs on-going incremental improvement of existing services.

The NHS have tested and utilised a wide range of improvement strategies in the quest to create faster, more effective change. This has included Lean and Six Sigma, both of which have delivered promising results, particularly when combined with other tools and techniques. Pioneers are undertaking early testing of the approach. The latest endeavour involves the integration of the two into an approach "Lean Six Sigma for healthcare".

Lean is an approach that seeks to improve flow in the value stream and eliminate waste. It is about doing things quickly. Six Sigma uses a powerful framework (DMAIC) and statistical tools to uncover root causes to understand and reduce variation. It is about doing things right (defect free).

A combination of both provides an over-arching improvement philosophy that incorporates powerful data-driven tools to solve problems and create rapid transformational improvement at lower cost.

The key is to find the optimal combination of both approaches. For example, adopting the Lean idea of focusing on what adds value and then using Six Sigma tools to help understand and reduce variation, when the value stream is agreed.

Industrial engineers invented both Lean techniques and the Six Sigma approach to process quality. Lean is a strategic approach to change and improvement. Focusing just on the tools at an operational level and reducing costs, will not obtain the full benefits.

Lean means "using less to do more" by "determining the value of any given process by distinguishing value added steps from non value added and eliminating waste so that ultimately every step adds value to the process".

It is relentlessly focused on the work and by definition the strategy becomes: focus on the work, learn from it and improve. That is your strategy. The strategy is simply to learn. Not understanding Lean and applying tools in isolation leads it to be a cost-reduction exercise.

We summarised the main criticisms of Lean as:
- Lack of consideration for human factors.
- Lack of strategic perspective (at least until recently).
- Relative inability to cope with variability.
- When Lean means laying off people.
- When people think Lean is only for manufacturing.
- Lean only works in certain environments; but it is more than manufacturing process design (a strategic approach).

The main criticisms of Six Sigma are summarised as:
- System interaction not considered; uncoordinated projects.
- Processes improved independently.

- Lack of consideration for human factors.
- Significant infrastructure investment required.
- Over detailed and complicated for some tasks.
- It is the new flavour of the month.
- The goal of Six Sigma (3.4 defects per million opportunities) is absolute; but this is not always an appropriate goal and does not need to be adhered to rigorously.
- It is only about quality.

Lean and Six Sigma are process based improvement methodologies. Both were developed in manufacturing environments. Both have proven their effectiveness. Proponents of both can point to numerous, and dramatic success stories.

Current emerging trends are indicating that integrating the best elements of both methodologies could help healthcare deliver strategic and operational objectives.

### NHS Experience

Lean techniques, such as value stream mapping, have been used in the NHS since the mid 1990s, largely through episodic Kaizen events or by combining Lean tools with other improvement approaches. Increasingly in the NHS, Lean is being utilised on a much more systematic basis, with a number of healthcare organisations stepping up to focus on organisation-wide value systems to achieve their strategic goals.

The starting point for the Lean Six Sigma initiative was a Six Sigma pilot programme which was set up on a countrywide basis. The programme was externally evaluated by AA Global Sourcing. This demonstrated that Six Sigma has both strengths and limitations as an improvement methodology for healthcare. NHS has had a lot of discussions about the positioning of Six Sigma, either as a comprehensive business strategy, or a toolkit. They reflected on whether Six Sigma has validity as a stand-alone approach to improvement. One of the key issues has been whether the basic premise of Six Sigma works in healthcare. That is, to what extent they can take an existing clinical process, apply a variety of analytical, measurement and improvement techniques and improve its sigma score to a level where the process is virtually "defect free".

They analysed the sigma scores in the projects that were undertaken as part of our Six Sigma programmes. They identified the baseline sigma scores for projects on a range of clinical processes across the whole country. The mean baseline sigma score of the projects was 2.0 and the median sigma score 1.9. This means that the clinical processes were defective more than 30% of the time. The lowest sigma score was 0.4 which meant that the process was defective 86% of the time. NHS concluded that this range of baseline sigma scores challenges the Six Sigma proposition that they can take an existing process and improve it to make it defect free.

Our hypothesis, based on these and other Six Sigma projects in healthcare, is that many clinical processes are intrinsically ineffective. The latest large study in US healthcare quality delivered to adults in the United States concluded that the "defect rate" in the technical quality of American healthcare is approximately 45%. NHS concluded that it is unlikely that they can systematically improve clinical processes to get a higher sigma score. NHS needs to redesign the basic process first.

This experience was a main driver in NHS decision to combine Six Sigma with Lean methods. This combined approach is gaining credence in manufacturing and service sectors globally. If we can use Lean methods to identify our value streams at a macro level, we increase the potential to design better basic processes that are more likely to benefit from Six Sigma. It is too early to synthesize the data on the outcomes of the Six Sigma projects within NHS. However, the early results that they have seen so far indicate that the teams have had success in improving sigma scores by one or two, but nowhere near a "defect free" level of performance. Lean Six Sigma gives NHS the opportunity to get the basic processes right (through Lean) then take the variation out of the process (Six Sigma).

While Lean and Six Sigma were developed separately, they have similar goals and approaches. The approaches complement each other. Lean Six Sigma is a strategic approach to change. It works best when it is used as a mechanism for achieving strategic improvement goals. Value streams and value systems transcend existing organisational and departmental boundaries. The tools of Lean Six Sigma can be utilised for departmental specific improvement projects but the biggest gains can be made at an organisational or system-wide level.

Never brand an improvement initiative by its methodology. Ambitions to be a "Lean Six Sigma Hospital" won't be achieved. Methods and strategies need to be behind the scenes of the goal of better health and healthcare.

Focus on results. Success is contagious. Improvement methodologies lose their credibility if they take too long to produce results or if they are too difficult to implement. Lean Six Sigma allows us to get results quickly and to tackle difficult systemic issues as well.

Link Lean and Six Sigma approaches with other tools for change. Engage the staff and change agents. With 1.3 million employees the NHS has a lot of brain power, experience, and common sense. Engagement helps to achieve success. No change process will work without active senior sponsorship, particularly by clinical leaders.

Some additional resources may be required in the short term to support the transition to this strategic and operational approach.

Measuring and understanding variation within a system has been a powerful way of influencing people's behaviour. This is a continuous approach, we need to educate, listen and create an environment receptive to continuous improvement.

# Chapter 7: Six Sigma Common Questions and Answers

What is the definition of "Six Sigma?"

Six Sigma is a systematic and statistically-based process to reveal defects in performance, driven generally by customer specifications. Six Sigma methodologies aim to reduce the variation and "non-value added" activity in clinical and business process which give rise to long cycle times, high cost and poor outcomes. A process that operates at true Six Sigma levels is producing acceptable quality levels over 99.9996% of the time.

Is Six Sigma a realistic goal for healthcare?

Although many healthcare processes cannot achieve such ambitious goals as implied by Six Sigma, this does not diminish the importance of the techniques. Six Sigma methodologies can substantially improve the performance of most processes, and a Six Sigma project that moves a "2 sigma" process to a "3 sigma" will have improved the performance of that process by nearly 450%.

Where does Six Sigma fit in healthcare?

Across a fairly limited number of initial pioneers we have documented nearly one hundred different Six Sigma projects that have delivered substantial gains to the organizations sponsoring the project.

Typical projects include:

- Emergency Department patient flow and cycle time.
- Operating room patient flow and cycle time.
- Laboratory and Radiology cycle time.
- Billing, coding and reimbursement.
- Supply Chain Management.
- Referral Authorization.
- Antibiotic Administration.

More than this, however, has been the significant impact that Six Sigma has had on the culture of the sponsoring organization. Six Sigma creates restlessness with the status quo, and a compelling force to improve how processes perform.

Why is Six Sigma gaining such attention?

There are likely a number of reasons why Six Sigma has gained so much recent attention, but none are as obvious as the struggle for healthcare organizations to overcome challenges related to quality and cost, and Six Sigma's ability to serve both goals equally and effectively. Furthermore, healthcare organizations have been frustrated by previous efforts to improve organizational effectiveness, as any incremental gains they achieve are quickly offset by incremental reimbursement cutbacks, incremental workforce shortage, and gains that are offset by other poorly performing departments. Healthcare executives have recognized that incremental gains are not enough to compete effectively with other organizations improving at the same rate, and that only "breakthrough improvement" will relieve pressure on margins and allow for the organization to take the lead in their market.

Where is Six Sigma in use within the healthcare industry?

More recently, blood banks have recognized the benefits of Six Sigma, a testament to its potential since blood banks are already held to extremely high standards of quality. More recently, providers and payers have adopted the principles. Many outside experts in Six Sigma believe it can have a greater impact in healthcare than any other industry.

What kind of track record and "ROI" has Six Sigma established in healthcare?

The typical Six Sigma project in healthcare has delivered an average of $500,000 in annualized savings. The key to Six Sigma's impressive gains is its ability to "do more with less" and to re-deploy critical human resources where needed the most.

If the ROI from Six Sigma is so compelling, why aren't more organizations adopting it?

Fear of the unknown. Six Sigma remains a mystical technique until healthcare organizations take the time to understand its comprehensive framework. Healthcare leaders may fear their ability to gain consensus around the use of Six Sigma; they may be concerned that it is a potential "passing fad," or too complicated to be effectively learned and applied by their staff. Finally, a significant impediment can often be the internal quality assurance infrastructure, which may feel threatened by the use of Six Sigma and its potential to overshadow their own accomplishments in the organization.

What are the key differences between Six Sigma and what I might be using now to address performance needs?

Six Sigma was not intended to replace traditional efforts at Total Quality Management or Quality Assurance, but the key differences between the methodologies have enabled Six Sigma to overcome challenges not sufficiently addressed with existing techniques.

Organizations that have implemented Six Sigma do not dispense with their existing TQM or QA functions. On the contrary, they either train these departments in the Six Sigma techniques or ensure close collaboration between these departments and Six Sigma practitioners.

Can a small or medium sized institution benefit from Six Sigma?

Absolutely yes; Six Sigma techniques have been effectively applied in hospitals with as few as 40 beds. Healthcare organizations generally operate most services 365 days a year, and the smallest providers still generates significant volume of activity which can be assessed and improved via Six Sigma methodologies.

Can Six Sigma be applied as an enterprise-wide initiative?

Six Sigma was designed as an enterprise-wide solution to management challenges. As many process improvement initiatives cross multiple departments, a Six Sigma practitioner inevitably must transcend different functions and departments in order to satisfy project requirements, effectively working in a "matrix" environment. It is this enterprise-wide focus that has allowed Six Sigma to accomplish such impressive gains.

Are there some departments that will benefit more from Six Sigma than others?

It was originally thought since Six Sigma originated in manufacturing, that only manufacturing oriented processes would benefit from the methodologies. However, a closer study of Six Sigma projects from that industry revealed that most projects were fundamentally "transaction" oriented, that is, dealing with the supporting processes of the manufacturer such as billing, receiving, accounts payable, supply chain management, etc. Since its arrival in healthcare, a transaction-oriented industry, the possible applications of Six Sigma have multiplied further. Not only has it been applied to the "back office" functions of the healthcare organization; Six Sigma has also been used to improve the performance of clinical processes as well.

Are there some areas where Six Sigma can have an immediate impact?

Six Sigma has its greatest impact on departments that are process-dependent rather than technology dependent. Having said this, however, Six Sigma can often improve the performance of departments that are evaluating technology investment, since no amount of technology can fix a broken process. Some of the other criteria used to determine if a project is qualified for Six Sigma include:

- Divergent views on how process is performing.
- Actual performance at 2 Sigma or lower.
- Suspected hidden factory and non value-added activities relates to defects (quality), cycle time, yield, and cost of use.
- Potential to reduce defect by 70% between observed and past performance.
- $175,000 initial and $500,000 future savings potential.
- Candidate for disruption - approximately 4-6 months duration.
- Minimum capital investment required.

What kind of training and support is required for Six Sigma?

Given the remarkable impact that Six Sigma can have on an organization, it may come as a surprise to learn that the implementation can be accomplished with little disruption to the organization. Organizations can select from a pure classroom training approach, or a combination of computer-based training (CBT) augmented with a minimum of classroom time. This approach is not only more economical, but allows each student to proceed at their own pace. CBT programs can be easily customized to accommodate the personality of the sponsoring organization.

Another popular approach is to combine training with an initial Six Sigma project, led by the consulting organization. This allows the organization to "train and achieve simultaneously," and can be an effective strategy to both secure buy-in while demonstrating the impact of Six Sigma to the organization.

The key to successful implementation of Six Sigma is strong and visible senior management support. This support is critical not only to overcoming natural scepticism of Six Sigma, but to allow its participants the free reign necessary to apply its principles once training is complete.

What are typical costs for implementation?

In the US and UK Healthcare providers should budget $10,000-$15,000 for pure classroom instruction per student and roughly half this amount if the combination CBT/classroom approach is used.

What are Six Sigma "black belts, greenbelts and yellow belts?"

A black belt has completed a rigorous course of study related to Six Sigma, including approximately 120 hours of instruction, homework and examinations, and culminating in a project that has been independently reviewed and certified as substantially conforming to the principles of Six Sigma. A greenbelt has similarly completed a course of study, though less time consuming and not involving as many of the advanced statistical techniques that might be necessary for more complex projects.

Black belts are trained to lead and conduct multi-disciplinary projects; Green belts are trained to support Black belt projects and to complete small scale projects within their own area of expertise.

Champions or "Yellow belts" is the designation given to senior executives that oversee the performance of Black belts within their organization. Finally, "Master Black belts" have completed a course of study to train on Six Sigma techniques, and they have also served as Black belts and have completed many projects. A typical Six Sigma organization will have a couple of Champions and Master Black belts, several Black belts, and a significant contingent of Green belts.

What are the advantages of integrating Lean and Six Sigma?

Integrating Lean and Six Sigma creates a win win situation. The philosophy of Lean provides the strategy and creates the environment for improving flow and eliminating waste. Empowered staff are encouraged to continuously improve to create value adding opportunities that otherwise would not be identified. Six Sigma helps to quantify problems, makes evidence based decisions (this prevents wasting time on anecdotal evidence), helps to understand and reduce variation and identifies root causes of variation to find sustainable solutions. Furthermore, it quantifies the financial benefits and savings. This helps to focus efforts in the areas that offer the most potential for improvement.

A combination of both can provide the philosophy and the effective tools to solve problems and create rapid transformational improvement at lower cost. Potentially, this could increase productivity, improve quality, reduce costs, improve speed, create a safer environment for patients and staff and exceed customer expectations.

How are Lean and Six Sigma similar?

Lean and Six Sigma are both customer-focused process improvement methodologies. They both follow the traditional quality improvement steps:

**1. Identify the project**
a. Nominate projects.
b. Evaluate projects.
c. Select a project.
d. Ask: Is it quality improvement?

**2. Establish the project**
a. Prepare a statement of goals.
b. Select a team.
c. Verify the statement of goals.

**3. Diagnose the cause**
a. Analyse symptoms.
b. Confirm or modify statement of goals.
c. Formulate theories.
d. Test theories.

51

e. Identify root cause(s).

## 4. Remedy the cause
a. Evaluate alternatives.
b. Design remedies.
c. Design controls.
d. Design for culture.
e. Prove effectiveness.
f. Implement.

## 5. Hold the gains
a. Design for effective quality controls.
b. Foolproof the remedy.
c. Audit the controls.

## 6. Replicate results and nominate new projects
a. Replicate the project results.
b. Nominate new projects.

How are Lean and Six Sigma different?
At one level, both Lean and Six Sigma are improvement methodologies. But as you investigate further, the contrasting aspects of the two approaches becomes apparent.

Lean is often seen as an efficiency approach which focuses on improving flow in the value stream and eliminating waste. It is more than this. Lean is a philosophy, not simply an exercise in eliminating waste. Lean is much more than episodic Kaizen (rapid improvement) events; it is a continuous improvement approach. It asks the question, "Why does this process exist at all? What is the value and the value stream?"

Six Sigma, by contrast, is often considered an effectiveness approach which focuses on the elimination of defects and reducing variation. It is seen as working best in an environment where there is variation. Six Sigma starts with "How can we improve this process?" It does not ask "Why does it exist at all?

Six Sigma is not just statistics, in its best incarnation; one integrates experience, historical, prospective, and data to make decisions. Six Sigma projects can last from hours to months, the methodology is not designed to tackle every problem in a set amount of time, but it is designed so projects do not take any longer than necessary.

Lean needs Six Sigma because; Six Sigma needs Lean because; Lean does not explicitly prescribe; it identifies waste. Six Sigma sub-optimises project set up and roles needed to processes (Lean applies a systems approach) achieve and sustain results. It provides a set of tools to understand. It improves process speed/cycle time problems and sources of variation. Lean does not recognise the impact of; it includes methods for rapid action (Kaizen) variation. Lean is not as strong in the measure and Six Sigma quality is approached faster if analyse stages of DMAIC lean eliminates non value-added steps

How are we integrating Lean and Six Sigma?

We have found that using around 20% of the tools achieves 80% of the benefits. We do this by focusing on the vital few things that will save time and maximise the impact gained. In healthcare settings, we have started to identify what value our customers are demanding and we have identified core value streams in healthcare. We have used Six Sigma tools to help us understand and reduce variation.

What are the lessons learned so far?
- Lean and Six Sigma are complementary not competing
- Start with goals and strategic intent; the quest for results should determine the improvement approach, not the other way round.
- Understand where Lean Six Sigma strategy is appropriate and where it is not.
- Test the approach.
- Focus on results.
- Engage staff and change agents.
- Senior Leadership must engage and actively participate.
- Resources are required to start improvement efforts.
- Use metrics to change behaviour for desired results.
- Educate, actively listen and encourage continuous improvement.

# Chapter 8: Six Sigma Allows Medical Professionals to Spot Variances

There are several different quality programs within the Healthcare industry. Six Sigma is just one of them, but has since become the leading quality management portfolio within this industry.

Six Sigma and its use in Healthcare is very beneficial. Its main focus is on reducing variability within standard processes. Six Sigma allows professionals in the Healthcare industry to appropriately and successfully figure the inconsistencies within their operations. It allows medical professionals the ability to detail processes within the field and quickly adjust and standardize them. If this cannot be done, Six Sigma still allows members within this field to come up with the best ways of dealing with and managing certain processes. For this to take place there must be a project leader. Preferably the department head or a team representative that is completely knowledgeable of the process in question. They will then be able to allocate and designate times and methods of completing each process successfully and further standardizing it for future use.

Over time, Six Sigma team leaders will be able to accurately figure, after taking several random samples during the process, and standardize the procedure. For instance, within the Healthcare industry, there is always the need to standardize the prepping process.

A lot of time is generally wasted since this procedure has no actual time slot or task list. After several days of noting the tasks within this process, Six Sigma leaders will be able to draft an accurate sample of what actually occurs during prepping and be able to create a routine which can be utilized by the entire staff. The use of Six Sigma within the Healthcare industry will thus allow medical professionals to spot variances and nuances within the process. It will then allow prepping to become more standardized and enable professionals to maintain this procedure in future applications.

Six Sigma within the Healthcare industry is rather effective as it allows for concentration on each individual issue, allocates time and effective measures to deal with them, and successfully brings about a standard method in the end. Six Sigma does have several advantages and disadvantages. One con to this method may be that the focus on just one process may alter another as Six Sigma does not normally recognize several issues at once. Additionally, each concept and approach will have its negative impacts. Six Sigma ultimately will lead to faster and more standardized processes and produce a more ideal end result.

Healthcare institutions will constantly have numerous priorities to deal with. When it comes to implementing the Six Sigma quality improvement strategy within this industry, there are guidelines which have to be followed in order to weigh the importance of each task and assign them accordingly.

Six Sigma is the perfect quality assurance program for the healthcare industry as it concerns prioritizing, itemizing and efficiently completely processes. Many healthcare institutions are using Six Sigma as a way to effectively improve their services in order to provide better healthcare to the general public. Successfully organizing and incorporating this management theory takes into account its methodology and theories and is highly dependent on a good foundation of training and certification.

Quality issues within the healthcare field can sprout from just about anywhere. The most common evolve around faulty equipment, lack of management or routine within a particular department, or there can even be problems throughout the organization as a whole. This process, when used and implemented correctly, can successfully alleviate procedural issues as they relate to medical care and operational issues like work-flow, registration, and billing.

First, Six Sigma asks that the "customer" be prioritized as the first step to successfully repairing an issue. Usually, within the healthcare industry, the "customer" could oftentimes be the patient, the nursing staff, the doctors, the stakeholder, the administrative staff, or the department manager. It all depends on the quality issue at hand and who will directly benefit from the changes that will be made. Of course the patients are the final customer when it comes to the healthcare industry, but since this process is a business theory, it needs to sometimes be viewed in a business light. In some cases, some problems are not prime candidates for Six Sigma.

This is because this process works best with complex issues with several variables involved that are repeated over and over. There are several other quality management programs that may help to solve simpler operational issues directed more towards facilitation, direction and building a consensus amongst all the people involved. Since most hospital procedures are repeated, it is a very viable option for most hospital processes, which is why it is so beneficial when it comes to the healthcare industry.

Six Sigma projects or the items that can be awarded as Six Sigma ready are numerous. Each healthcare institute has diverse problems which need to be rectified. Not all are the same but most can be summarized under general headings. For instance, most healthcare organizations tend to need aid with these types of projects:

- Aligning vital hospital problems with strategies in order to solve.
- Including a Black or Green Belt into a given project.
- Linking one project with another in order to bring about a combined and effective result.
- Finding out how feasible a resource or standpoint from data is.
- Figuring both defined goals with unambiguous parameters.
- Figuring the visible advantages for the customer.

These are just some of the common issues from within the healthcare industry. This quality management theory can be incorporated into the management framework of almost any intuition in order to bring about effective results and successfully allow for better healthcare processes. Because this particular industry deals with saving lives, quality should be the utmost goal for any manager who works within this jurisdiction. Six Sigma is the perfect framework to help increase both quality and customer satisfaction as a whole within the healthcare realm.

# Chapter 9: Applying Six Sigma Culture to Healthcare

From a quality control perspective, it is possible to use and apply six sigma culture to a changing healthcare sector. From the national discursions on the subject, the healthcare system is broken and in need of major repair. Striking a balance between cost, speed and quality is a challenge, but presents a perfect project for the six sigma methodology and way of solving problems.

The way it works now, doctors order $20,000 worth of tests on day one of a patient's visit. On the second day, treatment begins regardless of the fact that five or six of the tests had no bearing on the diagnosis. The doctor knew this going in. He or she was merely throwing everything against the wall to see what would stick, so to speak. That is not very cost effective. Within the six sigma culture, the method employed would be called the "5 why" process. In other words, one test would be ordered per day, evaluated the next, until all possibilities have been eliminated and the correct diagnosis determined. Doing the tests one at a time eliminates waste and money.

Because of the current system, most people in the US don't know how much their healthcare actually costs in the first place, so few take the time to haggle or look closely at bills or their statement of benefits from their insurance company. Employing six sigma culture and process control could in fact lower the cost, by smoothing out the system. This would be massive undertaking, but a necessary one if the goal is to eliminate the waste that has built up into the system over the years.

Healthcare is a very complicated system with few specifications for inputting patients into the equation. One of the specifications is pre-existing conditions, for instance. Variations exist in genetic, mental and physical conditions to name a few. The process that must be analyzed is completely out of control at this point, with many hands stirring the pot with overlapping responsibilities. This whole system is over seen by experts or doctors and other medical industry professionals, who also could be part of the problem. As with many problems with the process, any process, have the monkey wrenches tossed in at the front, by the ones in charge.

Someone once quipped that all quality defects originate with management. This is true of healthcare. Six sigma culture will uncover these problems, but can't guarantee that the system will be fixed or that management will listen

Healthcare organizations in the US are tight on their budgets today because of so many people that lack insurance and the numbers of emergency room visits or hospital stays that go unpaid. It can be hard for a hospital to remain open to the public, and lean Six Sigma can help to reduce costs so that the financial issues of our healthcare system are not such a burden. When you send employees to Six Sigma courses, they learn how to spend money wisely and how to cut wasteful expenses that are not necessary for everyday operations.

Processes can always be improved upon, especially in a hospital system. Patient care is vital when it comes to running lab reports and tests for the doctors. Many of these processes today are run by individuals at a computer. Human error is a factor, and it can mean the life of a patient.

Healthcare organizations are all about processes. Within the realm of healthcare, processes must run correctly, or a person's life could be on the line. When the job is as serious as this, you must look into a program that will help with structuring and making process perfect. The best option for healthcare organizations is Lean Six Sigma Training because it focuses on total improvement with reducing costs, improving performance and productivity, and ensuring everyone is entirely satisfied with their care.

When patients are satisfied with a healthcare company they are most likely to pay their bills. They will provide higher satisfaction scores by complaining much less as well. Lean Six Sigma can help a healthcare entity provide less wait times and variation for patients, an increased accuracy with prescriptions, and safer emergency departments. Patients will also benefit when a healthcare organization goes through Six Sigma Certification because the medical staff will make fewer errors and there will be less defects.

Physicians must be satisfied with a healthcare organization or they will go elsewhere to practice. It can be hard to find a good physician but by providing an outstanding facility with the best operations, it can help you maintain a good staff of physicians. Lean Six Sigma assures fewer physician complaints, reduced scheduling, and better working conditions. The clinical resource retention will increase which is a positive outcome also.

Patients are the most important factor with the healthcare industry but money is one of the controlling factors that need to be reduced as much as possible. Lean Six Sigma can help with a higher annual savings, less rework and waste, optimizing the overall supply chain management, and retaining clinical and administrative staff without the high turnover rates.

Healthcare organizations that put their staff through lean Six Sigma education programs benefit in many ways. Patients are happier, physicians want to work for you, and cost is as low as possible, while maintaining maximum productivity. Six Sigma courses can help with critical service issues and with automation of processes that might even be life threatening.

Perhaps no segment of American and UK enterprise presents more fertile grounds for Six Sigma and its DMAIC (define, measure, analyze, improve, control) methodology than healthcare delivery industry. Six Sigma certification and implementation into healthcare institutions presents the double barrelled opportunity of conserving resources and improving profitability, but much more critically saving lives and protecting and improving patient health and quality of life.

Although Six Sigma certification concepts were first developed and implemented in the manufacturing environment, its success in such places as Motorola and Boeing led to Six Sigma training migrating rapidly into the services industry. For a variety of reasons the implementation of Six Sigma concepts into the healthcare arena has been somewhat tardy and tentative.

In many cases the phenomenal improvements in the medical technologies have outpaced the management methodologies needed to deliver those advances to the patient in an efficient and resource conserving fashion. In recent years, though, the healthcare industry has recognized the power of Six Sigma and are rapidly adopting the measurable improvements it methodology can bring to many settings.

The Six Sigma error-free, defect-free, concept would seem to be a perfect fit for the healthcare industry. Chilling statistics in 2007 show an estimated 120,000 deaths per year resulting from medical errors; almost triple the number of deaths caused by automobile accidents. Medical error related deaths also outpace deaths from breast cancer, AIDS and a number other life threatening diseases.

Equally alarming, studies indicate that over one million patients annually receive additional injuries from medical treatment errors while in hospitals. From the human suffering perspective alone there is plenty of justification for aggressively introducing Six Sigma certification into all aspects of patient care.

Implementation of Six Sigma certification into the healthcare delivery system presents a somewhat different set of challenges than those of the manufacturing environment or in other service sectors. The quality of healthcare is strongly bound to the skill levels of the healthcare professionals and technicians.

These skills aren't so easily measured and controlled. Consequently, the application of Six Sigma principles to the healthcare environment is sharply focused on improving interactions between a number of already skilled and trained personnel. Improvements come through identifying and refining transactional processes that need to occur between the various specialties and skills and the controlling administration in delivering the entire healthcare package. In short, a Six Sigma approach to the healthcare industry places its emphasis on improving processes rather than refining skills.

It is likely that there will be some initial reservations about, and resistance to, Six Sigma certification from the staff of healthcare institutions. The time and expenses devoted to training for overall certification and the additional expense incurred when putting Six Sigma Green Belt and Six Sigma Black Belt trained personnel in place will seem excessive to many. It's essential that key doctors, nurses, medical specialists and the entire administrative/management team buy into the long term benefits of Six Sigma before a successful implementation can take place.

# Chapter 10: Failure Mode and Effects Analysis Use in Healthcare

Rather than guessing or using trial and error, Failure Mode and Effects Analysis (FMEA) method allows for a systematic analysis of particular processes and services. It will help determine potential failures, and then allow the process to be redesigned so that the failure risk is eliminated. Having a proactive means of evaluating concerns and issues is much more preferable than responding to the failures once they have occurred. FMEA itself was used by the U.S. Military back in the late 1940s, but didn't become a part of the Six Sigma Training until the mid-1980s. Then, in the early 1990s, the Six Sigma Process was seen to be a viable tool for healthcare improvements, which is when FMEA began being used in this capacity.

There are many different tools that are acquired in Six Sigma Training, but none that offer the same resources and approach as FMEA. It has a structured approach that allows the team to quantify certain processes to determine how they are potentially harmful and then to deduce an end result that eliminates or reduces that harm significantly. It is also a great process tool to use for Six Sigma Projects when setting priorities and when figuring out what needs fixed first is necessary.

Periodically, healthcare has been known to do root cause analysis based on errors or mishaps that occur.

Most times, this evaluation did not take place until the problem had already presented itself. Fixing the situation before it becomes an issue is the ideal way to do things. FMEA offers that exact chance for the healthcare industry to find and redesign certain processes or events that have inherent risks that need to be eliminated. Using Six Sigma Methodology to investigate, analyze, and redesign processes in healthcare can be advantageous to anyone who wants to make things better without waiting for proof that something needs improvement.

Healthcare has always been known to take the time to perform different analyses to fix various errors and defects in processes. However, the majority of these investigations aren't launched until after the problem has already occurred. Using Six Sigma Methodology and the FMEA principles of analysis, healthcare professionals can now redesign and correct processes and potential risk factors before they become a problem.

There are three main types of FMEA processes that are part of Six Sigma Methodology and Lean Six Sigma.
1. Process FMEA is designed to find defects within processes that are transactional, and the failure modes generally stem from causes that are identified within the process.
2. System FMEA is more specific in that it is used in early design and conceptual stages to analyze systems. The focus here is on potential failures that would be caused by design.

3.  Design FMEA is employed to find potential defects and failures that are caused by the design, and can come from causes that were found by a System FMEA.

There are three other less common variations, known as the FMECA, the d-FMEA, and the p-FMEA, which all add an extra step to the FMEA process or specify it further.

Given that there are so many different ways to use FMEA as taught by Six Sigma training, it is no wonder that the healthcare industry finds it so relevant and helpful in preventing errors in their setting. Doing a FMEA will improve the process as a whole, including the quality and safety of it. It also offers a structured means for identifying problems rather than just guessing at what could use some work. It offers documentation and finite evidence about the processes and what needs fixed. The main benefit of FMEA in healthcare, though, is that it increases customer (patient) safety, satisfaction, and overall wellbeing of everyone involved.

When it comes to preparing and updating your FMEA, there are a few guidelines to keep in mind. The Process Owner is the leader of the team, and the team should include people who know the process or are affected by it. The Process Owner is also responsible for updating the FMEA on a regular basis. These are the basic regulations of putting an FMEA team in place

Now that the overview, definitions, benefits, types, and preparation of FMEA have all been discussed, there are only a few things left to discuss. When you employ Six Sigma Training to do a FMEA, there are certain roles and responsibilities of those who are involved in the Six Sigma Process. There are also specific change techniques that can come in handy for FMEA projects that are facing adversity within the healthcare organization. Knowing these things is the final step in making the most of the FMEA Six Sigma Methodology for your organization.

Understanding how a cause can create failure, and how that failure can inherently create an effect on the customer (usually negative) is the key to successful use of FMEA in your Six Sigma Projects. The team members on any Six Sigma Process team will all have different roles and responsibilities to keep track of. The teams should be comprised of members from various areas of the organization that are affected or will be affected by the cause that launched the FMEA in the first place. Leaders and Process Owners are responsible for setting the stage to create an empowered team that has the initiative and time to complete the process.

FMEA teams involved in Six Sigma projects generally consist of 6-10 people. This can vary, depending on which process stage is being undertaken. The team should also have a leader, a record keeper, a time keeper, and a champion. The other members of the team should be knowledgeable about the process that is being addressed. It is helpful to have members that are good with quick decision making and team building skills, as well. Once the team is assembled, setting a few ground rules will set the stage and provide the circumstances under which people will be working.

For those who are facing adversity or a lack of acceptance from management or other employees within the healthcare organization, implementing a Change Acceleration Process might be helpful. This process can ensure that people become accepting and supportive of the FMEA Six Sigma Projects so that they can be completed without complication. This tool of Six Sigma Training will allow the team to demonstrate to the adverse parties how the FMEA for a particular process will be beneficial, swaying their opinion in the end. Once everyone supports the FMEA for a specific process, and the proper team is in place, the project can begin with the support that it deserves.

# Chapter 11: Is Six Sigma and Healthcare Organizations a Happy Marriage?

To a certain extent, healthcare organizations have been able to have better management of inventories, better purchasing processes, and improved customer satisfaction. This is often referred to as the low-hanging fruit of cost containment. Nevertheless, the need for improvement always arises.

The solution for this is the implementation of the Six Sigma training tools and techniques. In the healthcare sector, it is very imperative that further improvements are made.

In the healthcare sector, what matters most is not a performance based on averages, but the variance or the defects that the customers feel in the services given to them.

It affects the patients if there is any sort of defect in the services. Any department operating at lower levels of sigma means they have even larger defects.

Achieving a higher level means patient satisfaction for services, physician satisfaction, reduced waiting periods for patients, and increased revenues.

The DMAIC methodology can be useful in the improvement projects. Each step will bring in relevant data that will be able to help in bringing about improvement in the processes.

The Define phase is the most important as the objective of the project will be defined. The goal is to achieve higher revenues by improving the capacity and empowering the employees to sort out recurring issues. The Measure phase will see the measurement of the key drivers in the organization, such as procedure times, time between patients, etc.

In the Analyze phase, key relationships are identified. The most important phase of improvement is when the action plans and SOPs (standard operating procedure) are identified. The changes and metrics put in place are then used in the Control phase to make sure that the changes brought in are sustained and achieving outputs according to expectations.

If you consider an example of a cardiac catheterization lab, the customers here are the physicians. If a single cath suite is working in a single shift with all staff in the same shift, there may be something that the customer (i.e. the physician) expects. There may be a need to improve the time taken in the various stages of the cath procedure. If the study is undertaken, it will be discovered what steps can be done simultaneously.

You can use Six Sigma to identify areas for improvement and to set benchmarks to achieve greater value. From the administration point of view, it means success of the Six Sigma plan is improvement in revenues. Six Sigma can successfully deal with very sensitive and important areas of the healthcare industry and help bring about changes. The more measurable and objective the nature of data, the greater customer acceptance will be.

# Chapter 12: Improving Patient Satisfaction in Healthcare

In healthcare organizations, patients may be considered as customers. Keeping patients satisfied are considered as a top priority by many healthcare organizations. The traditional concept, that people need healthcare and will continue to use the same healthcare providers out of necessity, even if they are not happy with their services they receive, has been changing rapidly. A patient can now access more information on healthcare providers and can make more informed choices about their treatment. Quality is now playing a more important role as patients have started choosing healthcare providers based on quality of care and their level of satisfaction with the organization from their previous experiences. At the same time many hospital administrators have already started using the views and perceptions of their patients to organize their service and staff and for continuous improvement in the overall organizational performance.

Below are our three approaches to quality improvement in the Healthcare industry to improve patient satisfaction. They are

- Measuring the patient's perspective.
- Improving patient outcomes, and
- Using Six Sigma approach.

Regardless of which approach or approaches are used, support of senior level management is critical to the success of such programs.

79

## Measuring the patient's perspective

It is important to measure patient's perspective to the healthcare services. The services that patients receive is intangible, can't be physically viewed or touched like a manufactured product.

There are three ways to measure patient perspective.

- First method is to determine patients' preferences. This method involves qualitative measures, such as focus group, interviews, and surveys, to determine patients' desires and expectations about various healthcare services.
- The second method is patient's evaluation of the services they received. This method involves a questionnaire survey given to patients after they have received healthcare services to measure their level of satisfaction to the services received.
- The final method is to measure patient's perspective through reports of objective observations from the patient, such as how many times they were seen by a doctor during their stay in a hospital or how long they waited in the waiting room for seeing a doctor etc.

All three of these methods can provide valuable insight into patients' expectations of healthcare and their evaluations of services received. Patient views can be used to improve quality and gain business for healthcare organizations.

## Improving patient outcomes

Improving patient outcomes can also increase patient satisfaction. One example of this was in Dayton, Ohio where a community based approach was used to improve patient outcomes. In this community, five competing hospitals worked together to determine the best way to treat certain illnesses. The theory is that if many people work together, a better solution can be found than if one hospital works alone. In Dayton, the mortality rate from acute myocardial infarction declined from 9.68 percent in 1999 to 6.3 percent in 2002 after the community based approached was implemented.

## Using Six Sigma approach

Six Sigma is a powerful approach to quality improvement that can be used in healthcare organizations to meet needs and expectations of patients as well as to improve profitability and cash flow. A model of Six Sigma approach to healthcare quality improvement involves a six step process as described below:

- Define the goal and scope of the project, for example, improve patient satisfaction, reduce average patient waiting time, etc.
- Create a performance baseline to compare data evidencing errors, for example, develop a quantifiable Upper and Lower Control limits the average level of performance indicator of patient satisfaction (average performance level (+/-) Six Sigma of std deviation) against which performance can be measured., and for

81

patient waiting time, determine average waiting time expected by average patient, and its upper and lower limit.

- Continuously, monitor performance and collect performance related data using patient satisfaction survey, and for waiting time, design the patient appointment scheduling and patient waiting line system, implement the system, and continuously monitor the performance of the patient waiting line system.

- If the level of performance goes below the lower limit of expected performance level, then analyze root causes of the problem, solve (not just fix) the problem by removing the root cause.

- Implement procedures to remove the root cause of the problem and improve performance level of the system.

- Evaluate the performance of the system before and after implementation of the improvement to measure the results of the improvement (Evaluate patient satisfaction levels before and after Six Sigma, and for waiting line, measure waiting time before and after Six Sigma implementation).

In addition to increasing patient satisfaction, Six Sigma can be used in other areas of healthcare such as reducing medication mistakes, reducing diagnostic laboratory errors, and capability studies and improvement of various medical and surgical procedures.

# Chapter 13: Improving Pharmacies and Medical Billing Processes

There isn't much room for a mistake as a pharmacist because someone's life could be on the line. For example, if you accidentally fill a prescription for eye drops but give the customer ear drops instead, the person could go blind if they put the ear drops in their eye. Human error occurs all of the time and there is very little room for it in a pharmacy but it does happen. Six Sigma can help you analyze all aspects of the job and process of how prescriptions are read and filled to integrate better methods and minimize human error.

Pharmacies must regulate the drugs that are given to patients. They have to pay attention to people who are known addicts and the types of prescriptions they are filling for them. In addition to the regulation, pharmacies want to maintain a high level of customer satisfaction. This can be difficult if drugs take too long to fill and the people are left waiting. When prescriptions are called in over the phone, the customer expects it to be ready when they arrive to the pharmacy to pick it up. The processes for all of these situations are processes that a trained and certified Six Sigma Black Belt can improve upon. Lean Six Sigma provides methodologies of ways to eliminate bottlenecks in the processes. You will be able to identify which problems are causing a prolonging of insurance companies approving payment for a prescription. This way, the issues can be resolved and better processes can be put in place so there is fewer customers wait time and less time for you to have to be on the phone.

Six Sigma is very beneficial in pharmacy environments because of the control and regulation required with the industry. Making mistakes is unacceptable, but it does happen. As a pharmacist, Six Sigma training can help you minimize the amount of mistakes you make, and can teach you to find ways to improve processes so there is less waiting time for customers and a higher satisfaction rating.

Medical billing environments are very task oriented and process driven. The processes may seem time consuming, and there are most likely many bottlenecks within the organization that cause things to run slow at times. It can be frustrating when there are thousands of bills that need to be figured. A Six Sigma green belt is an excellent choice of training for any staff member. This type of certification will help a medical billing environment by finding ways to improve the billing processes and ensure total productivity.

Another way that Six Sigma can benefit a medical billing environment is by eliminating waste. It is usually waste and unnecessary steps that cause bottlenecks. Although every step completed may seem necessary, when you go through Six Sigma intervention it will help you identify those wasteful processes and resources that cause a slowdown in billing. Reduction in waste not only means that more can be done in a day but it also means that you can save thousands of dollars.

Increasing profitability is the primary goal of medical billing industries. You can increase profits when you can apply Six Sigma methodologies across an organization in every aspect. Medical billing can be improved to increase profits by using employees more effectively, automating processes, cutting costs, and more.

Six Sigma will teach you how to better an organization by making improvements. This type of intervention also includes information about how to successfully communicate a business strategy across the organization to other employees and how to integrate Lean Six Sigma into the billing environment also. You will also learn how to select the right statistical tools to help improve day to day billing functions.

# Chapter 14: Six Sigma Practical Applications in Healthcare Sector

## Six Sigma in Doctor's office

Most people that use Six Sigma Methodology do so to increase profits and returns on investments (ROI). However, there are many more benefits to be found through the use of Six Sigma, including everything from improved customer satisfaction to improved business practices and time management. When it comes to working in a doctor's office, Six Sigma Training can provide many tools to help create shorter waiting times, better patient flow, and even a better management of resources that will help cut costs.

For example, imagine that there is a doctor's office that sees 35 patients a day. Given that the office hours are 8 to 5, that is 9 hours of time in which to see these patients. That means that the office must get through roughly 4 patients an hour, giving each one about 15 minutes of the doctor's time. The first thing to notice here is that the scheduling might seem overbooked, and that they should scale back their appointments made every day. However, you can't control how many people are ill on any particular day, which is why you must make the most of every second.

Six Sigma could analyze the current trends of wait times, both in the waiting room and the exam room, to help create an idea of where processes are slowing down or which problems need to be addressed. It could also help to devise a schedule involving the use of a physician's assistant for minor issues such as colds and infections that simply need a once-over and some antibiotics. Six Sigma analysis shows that about 10 patients come in with minor care issues, which leaves 25 patients for the doctor to see in a day, which provides a much more reasonable schedule. The doctor can now see 2-3 patients an hour and spend more time with the ones that need the care the most, while the physician's assistant handles minor issues that don't need the doctor's time or attention.

Some people are not satisfied with seeing a PA when they visit the doctor, but in the effort to streamline patient care and provide services to all who need them, it may be the only solution.

### Six Sigma in Emergency Room

There are many places where process improvement can have a significant impact on business. However, there are few places like hospital emergency rooms where process improvement can actually affect people's health and lives as it makes a business more efficient. Six Sigma process implementation in the hospital setting is definitely going to provide many different advantages for those who are looking to improve things in any way that they need to. It doesn't matter if it's something as simple as paperwork processing or something more critical like patient flow and care processes, because there is room for Six Sigma in many places around the hospital emergency room.

There are many things to consider with Six Sigma implementation. You must first address the problem and determine that the solution can be found through a data measurement and analysis process like the one offered by Six Sigma. If this particular method does not suit your specific needs, then it will be up to you to determine the best problem solving tools to use. However, when Six Sigma is the process that you want to use, you can find many different advantages to using it. As far as practical application goes, here is an example of using Six Sigma in hospital emergency rooms.

Waiting rooms are known for being overcrowded, and emergency rooms are often prone to long waits for patients with non-critical injuries or illnesses. In order to improve patient satisfaction and overall performance, an ER wants to figure out a better solution for patient flow that won't involve as many steps and complications for patients coming into the facility. They know that the current average waiting room stay is about 20 minutes, and the room wait to see a doctor is about 15 minutes. They want to cut both of these down to around 10 minutes, and to do so without compromising patient care or hiring extra staff to handle the volume of patients.

They also know that there are doctors on other shifts that have virtually no waiting times and are often left doing nothing. A data analysis of the actual numbers using Six Sigma will allow them to re-distribute doctors around the emergency room, so that there are more doctors during peak hours and fewer doctors when they aren't needed. Just switching shifts and rearranging schedules isn't effective enough, because the data provided tells exactly where things need to be changed. This is one example of Six Sigma practical use in hospitals, but there are many other ways it can be used to benefit everyone involved.

## Six Sigma in Nursing Practise

Nursing is one industry, like many in healthcare, which needs to operate at peak performance all the time. When you use Six Sigma in other industries, increased profits or business success is usually the goal. However, in the healthcare industry, and nursing in particular, the Six Sigma Process is about a lot more than the bottom line. Patient care, and more importantly proper patient care, is critical and usually the focus of Six Sigma Projects in nursing. Whether you are dealing directly with patient issues or streamlining processes, it all revolves around better performance in relation to serving the patients that come into a facility.

Practical applications of Six Sigma within the nursing industry can vary greatly. One such example would be if you were to implement a Six Sigma Process to determine how to better utilize resources so that there are an adequate number of nurses available to serve all patients in a reasonable amount of time. If you have a situation where this is not happening, it can affect the entire operation of the facility, and that will always produce a negative outcome every single time.

If you take the opportunity instead to figure out exactly how your resources are being used through Six Sigma Process metrics, you can then re-allocate those resources in a much better way that will work for everyone.

Six Sigma will allow you to see exactly how things are operating on a numbers level. You can then use that data to come up with a plan for better execution of operations and procedures, including things like scheduling and other processes that take place within the nursing field. Using Six Sigma to improve the nursing world is a great way to have an analytical approach that stands on something more than just a trial-and-error process of finding what works.

There are instances where Six Sigma isn't always the right answer for every situation, but it can prove to be very effective when it does turn out to be the right solution. You simply need to step back and evaluate the situation as it stands, and then make the best decision as to how to handle it. If you find that Six Sigma is a potential tool that you can use, you can guarantee that you'll find many different advantages to using it. However, if you end up deciding that it isn't right for you, there is no harm done in that particular situation. As long as it is employed correctly, Six Sigma can be effective for process improvement in nursing.

# Chapter 15: Using DMAIC in Healthcare

In healthcare, the principles of the DMAIC Six Sigma Methodology can be used in many ways. To demonstrate the use of this principle, one of the examples will be noise reduction in hospitals. After all, hospitals are much more efficient and productive when the environment is quiet and professional. To start, the problem needs to be defined. In this case, noise is the problem that needs to be improved so that customers (patients) are more satisfied with their process of being in and staying in the hospital.

Once the problem is defined, it needs to be measured, which is the second step of the DMAIC Six Sigma Methodology. Measuring the noise will take a team of people to determine the different areas that the noise is coming from. With so many different areas in and around hospitals that can be responsible for noise, this will need to be broken down into sections. For example, set up a chart of which areas have the most noise problems so that those can be addressed primarily and even the location of the hospital in relevance to exterior noises that cannot be controlled. In this respect, uncontrollable noises would become accepted risks. All others can be placed on the charts for improvement.

Analyzing the noise is the next step of this Lean Six Sigma Methodology. The analysis of the noise includes charting where it comes from, how bothersome it is to patients, and determining how it can best be corrected. Along with the areas that are analyzed, times of day should also be taken into account. For example, measuring the noise in one area during peak hours and then again during off-peak hours will provide insight as to the cause of the noise and how best to correct the situation.

Lean Six Sigma Methodology points to improvement as the next step in this process. There are many different ways that the noise reduction can occur in different areas of the hospital. Take the time to plan a strategy that works effectively for the facility, even if it includes a variety of different noise reduction concepts and solutions. The more creative you are the better chance you have for succeeding at noise reduction. Finally, control the noise using the methods you have implemented for noise reduction, and you will see more satisfied patients and more relaxed and happy employees.

Our second example in this chapter will be the use of DMAIC methodology in Diagnostic imaging. DMAIC is designed for use in processes that are already in existence. It has proved very effective in improving the use of existing technologies, such as diagnostic imaging. In the define phase, the most common problems associated with a delivery process are identified and classified. In the next phase, problems that are specific to the healthcare organization are measured to assess their impact on the overall quality of services rendered.

In the 'analyze' phase, related business processes are analyzed for pinpointing the exact cause of the problem. This helps the management in making the necessary changes to the problematic delivery model. In the next phase, alternative solutions are studied and the most appropriate solution is selected. This selection is based on its ability to improve the efficacy of services delivered through the diagnostic imaging devices. In the last phase, effective control systems are put in place to ensure consistency of services. Control systems also help in checking the efficiency of the new service delivery models that were designed during the implementation stages of Six Sigma.

Diagnostic imaging refers to the use of medical equipment such as X-rays, MRI or magnetic resonance imaging, ultrasound and CT scans. These devices have proved very useful in diagnosing cancer, heart ailments and other fatal diseases. However, the effectiveness of such devices may be reduced due to the increase in the number of patients undergoing such diagnostic tests. Healthcare centres now have the option of implementing Six Sigma concepts in their delivery processes, to eliminate the common problems associated with increased patient traffic.

## Common Problems and Solutions

Six Sigma in healthcare centres can be utilized for overcoming common problems such as delays in diagnosis and treatment, departmental bottlenecks, increased duration of stays, patient dissatisfaction, referring doctor dissatisfaction, loss of outpatient business and loss of potential revenue. Although it is necessary to have the most advanced diagnostic imaging tools for optimizing performance, healthcare centres also need to have the proper systems and processes in place, to deliver safe and cost-effective patient care.

The most common approach involves the implementation of Lean Six Sigma tools and techniques, along with process enhancement tools that accelerate change and build acceptance. When Lean Six Sigma tools and techniques are applied in diagnostic imaging, it helps in time optimization, human and equipment resource optimization, improvement of service delivery structure, cost reduction and revenue optimization. All these are necessary for a healthcare organization that is aiming to deliver quality services and increase its revenues at the same time.

# Chapter 16: Data Warehouses and Six Sigma

Different companies operate their data warehousing in different ways. The components of the warehousing can be developed in house or by another party, or can be a joint venture between the two.

Often a company will focus on functional and business needs rather than performance constraints, a costly mistake which might mean missed deadlines and correcting errors, the very issues that Six Sigma training seeks to eliminate.

It is not new that modern day data warehouses are built for auto refreshing and/or compatible for at least real time updating. ETL, as extraction, transformation and loading of data flow is a very resource-consuming exercise in data warehousing.

The importance of data warehousing increases several times, considering the fact that data structures are both strategic and functional.

Even the real time refreshing of data becomes a daunting task with the refresh window getting clogged straining server resources, and there are additional factors which affect the performance of ETL.

Recent trends in data warehousing tend towards quantifying challenges within a family or group system. One way to do this is to organize each family according to a certain geographical location, with other subsets of data. The modules are developed right at the outset, with additional modules classified as they arise.

Six Sigma elements can be applied to software development strategy. Doing so means that potential problems can be identified at earlier stages, before they have a massive impact on output. Fine tuning deployment plans can also mean that data warehousing will return positive results.

While internal auditing means companies have a chance to analyse a slew of different processes, analysts cannot afford to lose sight of the fact that databases will always be intertwined with the system architecture they were built on. This will have an impact on the accuracy of their predictions within a business curve.

# Chapter 17: Six Sigma and Medical Transcription

In medical transcription, the thing that often makes all the difference between success and failure is the number of errors that might have been made by a transcription company. Most of the medical transcription projects are now outsourced to third party medical transcription companies and since clients expect a very high level of performance, these companies just cannot afford to make mistakes.

This is the reason why many of these companies have now started deploying time-tested and highly-effective quality control management methodologies such as Six Sigma. To get a better understanding of how useful Six Sigma actually is for the medical transcription companies, we will discuss some of its associated benefits.

## Significant Reduction in Transcription Errors

Since lives depend on accuracy, medical transcription executives just cannot afford to make errors while converting voice messages into electronic text form. Not to mention the transcription company's losses in case the errors exceed the acceptable limits, leading to the decommissioning of the entire project. However, since transcriptionists also have to meet deadlines, it often becomes quite difficult to achieve that perfect balance of productivity and quality. This is exactly where Six Sigma comes into play.

What Six Sigma does is that it helps businesses to identify the root cause that might have been responsible for the majority of errors committed by transcriptionists. Six Sigma focuses on the majority simply because it is just not possible for a company to look into each and every error committed while transcribing. After identifying the root cause, Six Sigma helps businesses to devise effective solutions that are acceptable to both the top management officials and the transcription executives hired by the company.

This way Six Sigma is able to solve the problems without affecting the morale and motivation of the employees.

**Improved Quality Control**

By combining statistical tools and techniques with advanced IT systems, Six Sigma enables transcription companies to keep an effective check over the final output. This certainly helps in improving output quality, but what is even better is that the objective is achieved without incurring huge costs. This becomes a possibility because most of the quality control systems are automated and have the capability to identify even the most difficult to detect errors and inaccuracies that might have occurred while transcribing.

Since no additional manpower is required for improving and maintaining the desired quality levels, medical transcription companies are able to make huge savings and that too without compromising on quality.

Six Sigma in the medical transcription business may be a relatively new phenomenon, but still there are many instances that prove the usefulness of Six Sigma in this highly demanding business domain. For proof, you just have to compare the "before and after" financial statements of the transcription companies that have implemented Six Sigma. You can then easily notice that the results after the implementations are far better than they were earlier.

# Chapter 18: Six Sigma and Clinical Results

It is not that Six Sigma cannot improve clinical results; it is just that Six Sigma in the healthcare sector is a relatively new phenomenon and as such not much has been written or documented on the subject.

Additionally, since healthcare centres normally avoid sharing their internal processes, it becomes quite difficult for outsiders to assess exactly how well Six Sigma is faring in the healthcare sector. However, since almost all the information that is available in public domain is positive, it can be said with certainty that Six Sigma does help in improving clinical results.

For better understanding, let us discuss some of the ongoing healthcare projects involving Six Sigma.

## Project for Reducing Chemotherapy Medication Errors

This Six Sigma project is currently underway at a prominent healthcare centre in London. The main objectives of the project include reduction of errors in chemotherapy administration, improvement in documentation, reduction of waste, improvement in patient satisfaction and improvement in the turnover of patients receiving chemotherapy treatment.

The project is currently in the 'Analyze' phase, which is the third stage of Six Sigma DMAIC process

(Define, Measure, Analyze, Improve, Control). The project may still be far from completion, but positive results have already started to pour in, evident from the improvements made in patient satisfaction and patient turnover.

Progress on the error reduction front is relatively slow, but the healthcare professionals involved are optimistic about the developments and are quite certain to achieve significant results in a month or two.

## Project for Reducing Bloodstream Infections (Bsis)

This Six Sigma project is almost in its final stages and the positive results achieved so far, vouch for the applicability and effectiveness of Six Sigma in the healthcare sector. The main objective of this project was to make improvements in the existing healthcare delivery systems so as to meet the prescribed BSIs standards.

The project was executed with the support of the healthcare staff, responsible for developing many innovative solutions such as the 'Infection Containment Kit', development of standard operating procedures, and creation of control charts for improved infection monitoring. These solutions were quite useful because they enabled the healthcare centre to achieve the desired results such as significant reductions in BSIs, increase in ICU capacity, and savings of over £450,000 per year.

All these benefits prove the point that Six Sigma is quite effective when it comes to making process improvements in the healthcare sector. Six Sigma in the healthcare centre may still be in its infancy, but considering the positive results that are being reported by healthcare centres and the optimism displayed by healthcare professionals, it can be said that in the years to come, Six Sigma will no longer be in the trial mode and will instead become a necessity in the healthcare industry.

That is good news for all the stakeholders, especially patients' for whom even a small clinical error can have fatal consequences.

# Chapter 19: Overcrowding Hospitals

There is an ever-increasing demand in the healthcare sector that leads to overcrowding of hospitals and increased customer complaints.

The Six Sigma Certification methodology can be put to good use in the healthcare sector to bring about process improvements with quick results. Improvements can be in common areas, such as cost management, improved services and high quality clinical services.

The major objectives are safety of patients, quality services, reduced turnover of staff and providing good working conditions as well as sufficient operating margins.

For example, in operating rooms and the process of surgery, there may be issues such as pre-op delays, unavailability of surgeons or even lack of some equipment. A Six Sigma project that applies Lean concepts to pre-op processes can help bring about major improvements.

Safer and efficient emergency departments can mean greater patient satisfaction. Kaizen events can be used to monitor equipment and supplies replenishment, staffing schedules, and anaesthetist availability.

The scheduling process, managed regularly as part of the Six Sigma culture, can help resolve issues like availability of rooms and the support staff.

Managing processes and information is a big challenge in healthcare environment, and there is a lack of data usage in a meaningful manner. The real issue or causes may be often ignored or forgotten in the rush to find urgent solutions.

Six Sigma helps define formal goals for healthcare organizations and a timeline to bring it into force. Well-defined goals must be connected to performance measures. Successful implementation of Six Sigma project in healthcare organizations depends on commitment of leadership and management along with a long-term vision.

The commitment of top-level management has to be communicated to lowest levels and training provide to the members. The returns on cost of training can be justified when results of first projects are evident. Process effectiveness improves and there is also reduction in defects and waste helping organizations to bring about savings.

By frequent communication of performance everyone in each area can connect to overall goals, be it nursing, housekeeping, billing, administration, or any other area.

## Overcoming Challenges

There are two typical areas; non-normal data distribution and discrete data which are a challenge to implementing projects. The critical areas where improvement is required can be overcome if enough focus is given on the training of members as well as achieving commitment from top management.

Unless the top management of a healthcare organization is committed to a Six Sigma certification initiative, it cannot address issues in their entirety. There are some areas where resistance is shown to changes or improvements and those have to be overcome with care of a Six Sigma Black Belt.

This can be done if top talented employees from the organization are selected for Six Sigma roles. Last but not least, it is necessary that project selection is done with perfect alignment to strategic goals. Finally, the emphasis has to be on achieving tangible financial results.

There is no one solution for all healthcare organizations. Each has its own set of problems, and each organization will have to work out its own Six Sigma certification solution that will maximize patient and employee satisfaction. They can then remain committed to providing the best services to the community.

# Chapter 20: Six Sigma and the Pharmaceutical Industry

We cannot conclude this book without looking into pharmaceutical industry. There are various IT factors when transitioning from an existing management process to a new one. In this case transitioning to Lean Six Sigma methodologies carry several IT factors.

The Six Sigma quality improvement theory allows businesses to continuously improve and change the industry in a positive direction. Because this process is so complex, businesses will require interoperable and flexible systems that will enable information to pass across the entire business. Lean Six Sigma allows information to flow and keeps management abreast with this information.

Within the pharmaceutical industry, mining data and interpreting it both seamlessly and quickly are very important aspects of Lean Six Sigma. With the help of this methodology's tools and theories, information is able to be transformed into data that can be used to outperform the competition. Having data as quickly as possible will also make it much easier to respond to and evaluate FDA inquiries. IT factors will support various tenets which are essential when implementing this quality improvement process.

**Tents within Lean Six Sigma include:**

The Integrity of Data

Data integrity is a very important aspect within the manufacturing industry, in which this business theory was first introduced. Pharmaceutical companies rely on trustworthy and accurate data in order to make wise and informed decisions. Pharmaceutical companies thus have various IT specialists and vendors who come up with solutions. Additionally, these companies will usually have various data files with customer and product information within separate IT systems and sites.

Within a lean environment, confidence is required in order to uphold the integrity of the entire supply chain. It requires a single strand of information which eliminates the chances of duplicated and outdated data. If this is not achieved, the industry runs the risk of high administration costs and bad decision-making.

Quality in the Manufacturing Process

Building quality in the manufacturing process is a key goal within Lean Six Sigma and enables the industry to successfully integrate the IT infrastructure. This further helps manufacturers to rely less on human checks and balances and more on automated ones.

Automated checks enable businesses to collect data much more quickly and are easier for regulatory agencies like the FDA to audit. In-line data is critical to quality within this theory, enabling pharmaceutical companies to manufacture defect free products, which is essential to this industry because lives are at stake when it comes to manufacturing medicines for people. Without the understanding of these quality improvement methodologies, this cannot be achieved. Quality within all industries is important, but within the pharmaceutical industry, it is essential. Because lives are at stake, quality, when it comes to creating and manufacturing medicines for individuals, is necessary. Any business theory that could help in this realm of industry is necessary to explore. Because the Six Sigma quality improvement theory boasts less than 3.4 defects per million opportunities, it is worth exploring in any industry, especially this one! As technology becomes more and more integrated into our daily lives, exploring these theories together is worthwhile for any pharmaceutical manufacturer.

# Chapter 21: Six Sigma Methodology in Biotechnology Industry

As we did in the previous chapter we felt it necessary to look into Six Sigma within Biotech sector because science is a constantly evolving field and it is not surprising how new concentrations tend to be added to the ranks. One of which is the biotechnology industry, which is considered an applied form of biology. Here are some of the most important contributions that this sector has brought to mankind.

The Biotechnology Sector of science, or 'biotech' like it is sometimes referred, is considered to be a third wave in the field of biological science. Thus, it is often characterized to be the representation of both the basic and applied fields of the science. Here, the gradual transformation from the use of both scientific principles and technology are witnessed. This is a very important field where biology, technology and engineering are used to create practical goods and services for mankind. Because the Six Sigma quality control method is often used in engineering settings, the theories carry over, and are also useful within the field of Biotechnology.

One of the most important components of this sector is referred to as 'red'. This pertains to the creation of drugs, medications, or antibiotics that are used clinically to make people better when they are sick. In this particular field, professionals study certain microorganisms with the hope of making it easier for man to combat deadly illnesses, epidemics, and diseases.

White or gray fields in this sector are considered to be related to industrial processes. This means that findings in this field are being used towards the production of products and materials other than food. One very common strategy within this field is to utilize microorganisms and other living things towards the production and composition of chemicals that are considered very important for industrial uses.

One of the most crucial contributions of blue biotechnology industry is the fact that its results allow people to be able to use lesser resources when performing various industrial procedures. This is specifically true if these procedures are compared to the traditional ones, wherein people will often have to utilize more resources to help achieve the same kind of scientifically relevant result. The blue sector of biotechnology is where the Six Sigma Tools and Theories fit in the most seamlessly. This is because they both have similar goals to get the most worthwhile work done with the least amount of resources in the least amount of time.

There is also the green field, where the main concern is the use of the technology to better accomplish agricultural processes. This may often involve performing experiments on how an organism (i.e. food) can be grown in certain environmental conditions. The propagation of a particular plant species will be easier despite the deficiency in the necessary elements to make it grow.

Another concentration of this field has something to do with the use of processes that concern the marine and the aquatic fields. Here, the techniques utilized will be used toward ameliorating common aquatic issues and marine conditions that need to be duly resolved.

In addition, the biotechnology industry can also be further subdivided into two specific concentrations. The first one pertains to the processes that are considered non-gene which utilizes tissues, whole cells, or individual organisms alone. The second is considered to be the gene type where professionals perform gene cloning, manipulation, and such other similar processes. No matter the subdivision, the Six Sigma Methodology's tools and techniques are very pertinent to this particular field of science. When combined and used together, the two can make great strides toward efficient scientific discoveries that will better our lives, our children's lives, and hopefully their children's lives as well.

# Chapter 22: Six Sigma Certification in Healthcare

All across the world, there are millions, if not billions, of professionals in the medical field. From nursing assistants, surgeons, general practitioners and other similar healthcare professionals. Many are unsure of what Six Sigma can help them achieve and how exactly to utilize this training in their field of work.

Six Sigma is especially beneficial within the business aspect of the healthcare industry. This method of completing projects successfully is especially advantageous to the healthcare industry. First, one will have to undergo training and later receive certification in their chosen course of study. This can be done in a variety of ways. Initially, because of the medical field's very busy work times and tasks, the easiest way to undergo training and receive certification will be via the Internet. Six Sigma certification can be applied for and attained in this way. This is probably the best way to go about receiving certification as online learning is done at a slower and more convenient pace perfect for persons within the busy medical field. Online certification will also not be as costly as applying for physical classes and onsite training seminars.

Many healthcare institutions are also already seeking Six Sigma knowledge. Many administrators are offering and making training accessible and available to their employees. Classes are usually conducted within the facility. Some employers even pay for training as a means to better standardize and ultimately benefit the business on a whole. For those who have not heard this management term thrown around the office, mentioning it to the head of a department, explaining and showing them how it works may provide the entire staff with access to lessons.

Six Sigma benefits the healthcare industry in many different ways. It is able to help individuals achieve more from the medical field than they could have without it. It allows them to make fast and accurate decisions. This process also enables individuals to figure and solve problems, processes and procedures faster. This will ultimately lead to more efficient work and may even save the hospital a few dollars.

Six Sigma has many other benefits within the healthcare industry so it is important to seek training and certification whenever possible. This industry is much more than a business or organization but a means to help, treat and better the lives of unwell individuals. Six Sigma allows medical professionals the tools to perform faster and make more informed decisions which will ultimately lead to better healthcare.

The healthcare industry is one where defects and mistakes are not and cannot be tolerated. A mistake could cost a patient their life. This means processes need to be in place and followed exactly how they are set forth to eliminate mistakes. A Six Sigma certification is the best requirement in a healthcare environment for employees dealing with critical patient information.

Although the Six Sigma Methodology may have been developed for a manufacturing organization, the good news is, it can be used in a healthcare organization in order to give the same added benefits. The healthcare industry is a service organization facing challenges everyday. Quality improvement methods are more difficult to implement in a healthcare industry. The comprehensive approach offered by a Six Sigma certification allows for the methodologies to be successfully implemented with positive results.

A Six Sigma certification provides the tools and resources required for a healthcare organization to manage effectively the interaction of information and the interaction of people in this critical environment. Processes can be easily transformed for total quality results and better productivity without the worry of critical mistakes. Many people in a healthcare environment are stuck in their ways because they are used to running the same processes on every shift. A change can be dramatic, if not cause anxiety to staff members. The Six Sigma certification shows management how to implement effective changes in a critical environment, such as healthcare, by creating motivated employees who are ready and willing for the changes.

Healthcare organizations are behind the times in managing people, documentation, systems, and other resources. This is because changes are so difficult to make in such a critical atmosphere. A Six Sigma certification program shows management how to create a long term vision and slowly work toward positive changes that can help reduce costs, increase productivity, and create an atmosphere employees are happy working in.

The Six Sigma certification program is designed to reduce waste and save money. Healthcare organizations can find different approaches to systems that save time and reduce the probability of making critical mistakes. This type of program is ideal for management in any type of industry including retail, manufacturing, industrial, service, and even healthcare.

The best thing a healthcare organization can do today is require management to undergo Six Sigma certification training with their staff. This will help management make positive changes to reduce waste such as unnecessary steps in processes, physical assets, and labour. New systems can be put in place to better healthcare operations to ensure mistakes are almost impossible to make. This will help create a safer environment for patients and improve employee morale.

Many healthcare industries have utilized the benefits of Six Sigma training as well. In the case of this industry, Six Sigma concepts can help in reducing quality issues which may lead to defects which can prove fatal, in extreme cases.

## Heading off Inefficiency

Medical and technological advancements mean that there is an increased demand and expectations put on medical care, with expectations going up in further in the future.

Unfortunately, ineffective management systems have meant that inefficiency is in fact on the rise, leading to lost revenue, user complaints, and crowded emergency rooms.

With Six Sigma training concepts and methods, the business processes within the healthcare industry can be streamlined. This will result in improved healthcare services to patients, with the focus being on human skills.

These skills can be difficult to quantify or control, so the Six Sigma approach proves effective as it focuses on both the human and transactional elements of a process.

There are challenges which are unique to implementing Six Sigma training within the healthcare industry, but the results are generally quite quick and always desirable.

## Improving Processes

The flow of information, along with the interaction between different people, is at the heart of quality and efficiency in healthcare.

A cultural shift in the organization can often serve to streamline both factors, which will in turn achieve strategic business results.

Instead of just looking at the task at hand, the methodology looks at improving all processes thus increasing the scope of all improvements.

Six Sigma training does this through the provision of tools and methods designed to analyze and change human performance, which is necessary in achieving significant long term improvements.

**Looking to the Future**

There are several steps within the Six Sigma certification process. Most notably, the system defines a vision for the future which helps to identify specific goals and look at ways to turn those visions into a reality.

To this end, goal plans are made and timelines set that state when current performance levels will be transformed to Six Sigma performance levels.

These plans are defined after documenting their effects on the organization's work processes (these might include the flow of information, surgical site procedures, patient interaction, and other factors).

When it comes to the groundwork for successful implementation of Six Sigma, there are a few requirements. Long term vision, commitment, leadership, management, and training are all building blocks necessary for success.

All staff, from doctors and nurses to administration, must be on board and trained in the various concepts and methodologies involved in implementation.

While the initial costs of implementation are high, management needs to keep in mind that the outcomes will result in many times more dollars saved than those spent.

# Chapter 23: Auditing and Six Sigma Certification

Innovation is encouraged throughout the Six Sigma Certification process, thus variabilities may occur that have an effect on the goals and outcomes of the project. The quality of deployment and the existing business structure are two examples of variable factors which can affect the outcome of Six Sigma.

In order to ensure that the project is being implemented as planned, then, Six Sigma teams need to perform regular audits. This process is similar to the assessment process which is conducted during the employment stage; at this time only qualitative checks are conducted.

The tools used in the audit process include checklists and questionnaires, which allow the people performing the audit to assess the existing status of the business process. This status will next be checked against the desired outcome or result of the deployment, things which are set ahead of time.

These standards are quite specific, and will be clearly defined at the opening stages of the deployment phase.

## Audit and ISO 9000

The audit process is yet another area wherein Six Sigma Certification and ISO 9000 are quite similar.

However, it is important to note that as with other aspects of the ISO 9000 process, Six Sigma audits tend to go a little bit further, while still using the same audit platform endorsed by ISO 9000.

The extra steps usually include the voice of the customer, tacked on to Six Sigma audit. The key to any audit, of course, is ensuring that the checks are completed thoroughly and accurately.

During a Six Sigma audit, descriptive charts in the form of checklists are used on every single aspect of the project. The individual checklists are carefully prepared, with each one applying to a specific business process or activity.

The lists are prepared at the initial stages of the project deployment process.

**Checklists**

Standard operating procedures, or SOPs, are the foundation for the process checklists used in the auditing process.

The goal is for the auditors to determine how well a particular process has been implemented, and how well that process is being followed.

The SOPs used for the checklists are determined at the commencement of implementations, and are question oriented.

There is a scale used, developed ahead of time, which enables auditors to rate the processes by the different answers which are obtained.

Answers to the various questions on the checklists will also be summarized and recorded on the checklist. For example, a business process related to a dispatch system may be up for auditing.

In this case, the process variations that have been recorded in the operator's log will be revealed during the audit. Any variations will be compared to the predetermined standards, so that the extent of the problem can be determined.

With the data representing the deviations in hand, the causes of those deviations can be discovered.

It is important to note that while the Six Sigma Certification audit is quite reliable when it comes to checking the progress of Six Sigma implementation projects, the scope is limited to existing business goals and objectives.

## Audit Scope

In this way, the Six Sigma audit differs from the rest of the Six Sigma Certification methodology. The audits therefore cannot be used to improve upon existing quality levels achieved by the organization.

Instead, the audit will measure and analyze customer feedback in terms of the changes made during the implementation.

If the feedback is positive, the processes are maintained. Negative correlations between feedback and effected changes will mean the process is set aside, or marked for further improvements.

While the scope of Six Sigma Certification audits is limited, they do provide a useful tool when it comes to measuring the success of implementation projects.

Without these audits, errors may occur along the way which may damage the entire project.

# Chapter 24: Conclusion

Understanding, meeting and exceeding patients' needs and expectations, a healthcare organization can improve patient outcomes, and at the same time can remain competitive by cutting costs and improving quality. Six Sigma is relatively new to the healthcare industry so there are more opportunities that can be explored.

Patients or prospective patients could be used as team members on Six Sigma projects. An outside perspective can also be beneficial in determining what patients want and do not want. For example, some Six Sigma projects may look into minimizing patient length of stay in hospitals after a certain procedure. Most patients want to go home as soon as possible; however some patients might not be able to take care of themselves or might be in too critical of a condition to risk leaving the hospital. This is where a patient representative on a Six Sigma team could be beneficial.

Six Sigma may also be applied to the triage process in emergency rooms. Patients may be interviewed when they arrive at the emergency room to determine the extent of their illness and their priority to see a doctor. This process could be streamlined by the use of Six Sigma so that critically ill patients can quickly see a doctor and not get stuck in the triage process.

Six Sigma can also be used to decrease the time patients spend in the emergency room by getting patients admitted to hospital rooms or discharged quicker. Patient rooms are more comfortable than the emergency room and it is also very expensive to stay in the emergency room. Also, this could allow emergency rooms to treat more patients.

Hospital laboratories are another area of healthcare that could benefit from Six Sigma. Laboratory turnaround times can be lengthy and the workload could be sporadic rather than constant. Six Sigma can be used to help manage these issues by optimizing resources. Laboratory procedures can also be investigated to ensure that unnecessary steps are minimized while still obtaining the desired results.

Six Sigma can also be used to optimize the scheduling of time for the testing equipment such as MRI machines and the resources to operate these equipments. Also, scheduling can be done in such a way that patients most in need of the services can be scheduled giving higher priority. The Six Sigma approach can also be used for designing new hospital facilities and also remodelling existing ones. The flow of patients should be considered for facility planning and layout of operating rooms, laboratories, and waiting rooms, considering factors such as convenient locations for the patients, doctors and visitors. A patient voice of customer study may be done so the décor and layout of patient rooms are comforting and pleasing to patients while remaining functional for doctors and nurses. Operating room layouts may also be optimized for surgical procedures.

Thus, Six Sigma approach to quality and productivity improvement can be successfully used in healthcare industry similar to the ways Six Sigma approach is being used successfully in manufacturing industries.

Lean Six Sigma combines two approaches which have synergy; both approaches require a process focus, and both include customer drivers, either to define what needs to be improved (Six Sigma) or to define value (which then drive process improvement). Six Sigma focuses primarily on reducing variation, whilst Lean focuses on improving flow in the value stream and eliminating waste, although both may have similar secondary effects.

An effective combination of both approaches includes the value-maximising philosophy of Lean, underpinned by data-driven methods in decision making (from Six Sigma) focused on the customer (from Lean). All incentives and measures are reviewed (using Lean) to ensure global optimisation and minimisation of variation (from Six Sigma) would be a part of this.

The full benefits of Lean Six Sigma will only be realised when applied at both strategic and operational levels, with universal application only at the strategic level. Application at the operational level results only in cost reduction, whereas application at the strategic level results in wider benefits for the organisation.

The NHS in the UK has found Lean and Six Sigma as a promising improvement methodology that incorporates the best of Lean and the best of Six Sigma. The two approaches to enhancing value, eliminating waste and reduce variation can be used in a complementary rather than in a competing way.

A pragmatic approach is required; use Lean and Six Sigma where necessary, or use Lean where Lean is necessary or Six Sigma where Six Sigma is necessary. Combining common sense (Lean) and common science (Six Sigma) offers the potential to achieve uncommon results.

Keep improving!!